Are You Considering the Guitar?

The Guitarist's Lifestyle

Timothy Nicholas Sarno

iUniverse, Inc.

New York   Bloomington

Are You Considering the Guitar?
The Guitarist's Lifestyle

iUniverse books may be ordered through booksellers or by contacting:

iUniverse
1663 Liberty Drive
Bloomington, IN 47403
www.iuniverse.com
1-800-Authors (1-800-288-4677)

*Because of the dynamic nature of the Internet, any Web addresses or
links contained in this book may have changed since publication and may
no longer be valid.*

ISBN: 978-1-4401-2771-7 (pbk)
ISBN: 978-1-4401-2772-4 (ebk)

Printed in the United States of America

iUniverse rev. date: 3/3/2009

To my grandfather George Kuborn; my mother, Gloria Barton; my cousin James Lighthiser; and my friend Louis Vasquez

To my life partner and lady, Barbara Cacioppo, and her son, Dylan Dupasquier, who produced all the cool artwork

To my many students, who, through their many questions, made me realize it was necessary to write this book

Thank you all for your support. Without it, this knowledge would have been unavailable to future generations.

Contents

Preface

It was the summer of 1964 when I first expressed an interest in playing guitar. I had just turned fourteen. My grandfather, a banjo player, heard of this and presented me with an old ukulele. The ukulele was one of the forerunners of the guitar. He thought it would provide me with a good way to start out. Like a typical teenager, my heart was set on playing rock-and-roll guitar. The whole family urged me to learn how to play that ukulele. In spite of my feelings, I learned how to play it. At the end of that summer, I sold my pool table and bought my first guitar and amplifier. The guitar was an inexpensive department store variety. The strings were so high off the fretboard that after playing for a while, I thought my fingers would fall off. Still, I played that guitar to death.

When I think about being a guitarist for over four decades, it's hard to believe. Although my interest in rock and roll has somewhat faded, I still keep up with playing the guitar.

These days, my forte is movie soundtracks, new age, space, trance, and occasionally some rock tunes. After growing bored with standard tuning, I started writing in open tunings. About ten years ago, after purchasing a guitar synthesizer, my musical taste changed, and I became interested in writing soundtrack music.

When I started teaching guitar again, I realized that students required other information in addition to learning how to play the guitar. All those years as a musician had given me other knowledge that was just as important. This information wasn't taught through conventional teaching. Some of the details were only minor, but all of them held merit. I believed that this information should be a prerequisite to learning guitar. It would prevent costly pitfalls and might save the new student from setbacks and discouragement.

This presented a predicament: how could I impart this knowledge without impinging upon the lesson or my own time? Necessity is the mother of invention, and writing this book presented the answer to my dilemma. With this information available to my students, I would be able to teach with a clear conscience.

The expansion of this book made it possible to include the people who have always considered playing the guitar but are uncertain about whether they want to try. Now everyone has the opportunity to make an educated decision about playing guitar. I wish this book had been available when I first considered playing guitar, if for nothing more than the information provided here. I believe guitar had already captivated me as a child.

In a Word

It gives me great delight to be able to pass on this knowledge to other generations of potential guitar players.

Here are a few words of inspiration: Hold on tightly to that curiosity, and dream. Following through could present a great new opportunity. One can never guess where it will lead. The next guitar god or goddess might be you. In the beginning, I couldn't have guessed the heights my ability would achieve.

The Amazing Guitar

Here is a brief history with some interesting facts about the guitar. Stringed instruments such as the lute date back to ancient Egypt, and to extreme antiquity in Persia and Arabia, which had plucked instruments. The acoustic guitar came to America in the mid eighteen hundreds. The very first electric guitar featuring a solid wooden body was made out of a railroad tie and named "the Log. Lester Polfus, whom guitarists know so fondly as Les Paul, with his famous Les Paul guitar, created this experimental guitar. Another instrument maker, Leo Fender, followed Paul's lead and introduced three solid-body models in the 1950s: the Broadcaster, the Telecaster, and the Stratocaster. The latter two are still favorites of current rock-and-roll players.

Originally, the guitar only had four strings; the fifth and sixth strings were a later addition. The two extra, larger bass strings lent to a richer, full sound. This improvement enabled the guitarist to play bass notes in accompaniment with chords. Nowadays, it is hard to imagine a four-string guitar. I use the fifth and sixth strings extensively. Guitars with seven or eight strings were common in the later nineteenth century, and seven-string guitars are still widely played in Russia.

To the new student, the fifth and sixth strings make the guitar seem very complicated. The complexity lessens after learning that the first and sixth strings are both E strings, having the same notes on the fingerboard, three octaves apart. With this perspective, the fifth string is really the only new addition. The fifth or A string bridges the sixth E string to the fourth D string, enabling a smooth transition when playing note progressions. These extra bass strings also add lower octave notes for scales and fuller-sounding chords.

The guitar is one of the easiest instruments to learn. It is also considered one of the hardest to master; therein lays its irony. Learning to play any instrument presents a new dimension to one's lifestyle, bringing entertainment, enjoyment, and personal fulfillment. It doesn't matter whether you learn simple, open country chords for sing-along or become a master guitarist who dazzles a captivated audience.

Even after playing for over four decades, the guitar still holds new surprises for me and never ceases to be amazing. I have seen many new innovations, such as new types of guitars, effects boxes, synthesizers, and even new playing techniques. The guitar also seems to have inexhaustible versatility. I find it absolutely the most fascinating out of all of the musical instruments. I can't talk enough about what the guitar has brought to the table.

I have spent a great deal of time and money, with little monetary gain but with no regret. Playing the guitar offers so many other rewards: the feeling of fulfillment, the accomplishment of learning how to play, playing new music, writing music, the entertainment value for yourself and others, enjoyment of playing, and pride and satisfaction in performing well. I believe that playing guitar can have a meditative quality.

Thinking of investments brings to mind an amusing personal anecdote. My friend Brian wanted us to record our own CD. He already had the recording equipment, but I would need to invest in new gear. My share required a large chunk of money. Admittedly, I was somewhat skeptical, but the opportunity to produce my first CD was a strong incentive. However, I was still ambivalent. After months of being persuaded, I agreed. On our way back from the music store with my new gear, Brian sheepishly posed some questions. Was I worried about making the investment? Would I be upset if we never produced a CD? After my look of consternation, he smiled and told me not to worry. Much to my dismay, that CD was never recorded.

But my investment in a guitar synthesizer has proved its worth many times over. This marvelous piece of technology opened many new horizons while awakening my ability to compose in many new genres. I went from being disgruntled to eternally grateful. It was a blessing in disguise. The synthesizer opened up new venues to market my talents. Each time, playing using all of the various settings was like a breath of fresh air, the dawning of a new musical era. I was ecstatic over the abundance of instruments and sound patches at my fingertips. It felt like becoming instantly musically unbound. My enthusiasm for the guitar reached a higher level. The innovation this time was in how the strings were utilized.

A guitarist using a synthesizer produces a more natural sound by using different attack techniques; this makes the sounds superior to that of a keyboard synthesizer. I must have been destined to acquire this synthesizer. Okay, enough—this is starting to sound like an advertisement.

If you would like an in-depth history of the guitar, there are books at your local library, like *The Complete Idiot's Guide to Playing the Guitar,* by Fredrick Noad, or *The New Harvard Dictionary of Music.*

Considering the Guitar

To begin with, you must realize and consider the initial expense. This involves not only expenditures for the instrument, but also for the accessories, lessons, and books, as well as learning and practice time.

Despite the challenges you face along the way, most people, with a little perseverance, can learn to play guitar. The time involved in learning how to play will vary for each individual. You will need to learn to be patient with yourself. Some people will pick up on the guitar in weeks, while others may take months. Mostly it will be determined by how much enthusiasm you possess.

After giving the guitar several attempts, you may decide that it's just not for you. Maybe it is time to throw in the proverbial towel, but first ask yourself this: What was your initial goal? Was it only for self-amusement, or maybe learning enough simple, open country chords for a sing-along? If so, give it a few more weeks. You'd be surprised by how often people believed they had given their best attempt, and then all of a sudden, their ability made a quantum leap. This is not that unusual. This has happened to a lot of people, including myself.

Is it your aspiration to join a band eventually? If so, what type of band? If it's rock and roll or blues, you might just need to learn the pentatonic scales and simple open and bar chords. If you become serious about playing in a band make a commitment. Learn music theory and how to read notes; learn scales and the various forms of chords. This is certainly necessary for playing in an orchestra, or in wedding bands, big bands, or jazz bands. After all, you have gone through all the work of learning the pentatonic scales and various chords; additional chords, scales, notation, and theory aren't that much more work. The standard major and minor scales are only two more notes in each scale. You might be remembering how much work it was to learn how to read. This is a bad comparison. Learning notation isn't difficult, though it won't be covered here. There is plenty of material at the library and in stores. Instead we will cover information not generally found in those books.

Whenever starting a new endeavor, it's important to allow the necessary time in order to make a fair assessment. This enables you to decide what level of commitment to pursue. Remember, the more effort you put in, the more you will get out of it. My personal motto is, "Anything worth doing is worth doing well."

Here are some words of encouragement. I use to dream of the day when I could play as well as my idols. Being able to do so is a fulfilling, fantastic feeling. The effort, energy, and expenses I put forth were well worth it. Listening to music enriches one's life. After becoming a musician, music becomes much more, opening a doorway into a whole new world. Songwriters experience much the same feeling. They observe and absorb life-gathering moments, creating the vocals that a singer sings. It doesn't matter whether you are a professional or play for enjoyment; playing a musical instrument enriches one's life. Hobbies are fun but often change. Playing an instrument, such as the guitar, can stay with you for a lifetime. Even if you don't play for a while, you can jump right back into it. It's kind of like riding a bicycle; you never forget how to play.

If age is a concern, don't give it a second thought. Edward Taub at the University of Alabama studied the region of the cortex responsible for evaluating the tactile input from the fingers. Comparing non-musicians to experienced players of stringed instruments; he found no difference in the brain regions devoted to the fingers of the right hand but a huge difference for the fingers of the left hand. If we drew a picture of the hands based on the amount of brain tissue devoted to analyzing touch, the musicians' left-hand fingers (which are used to control the strings) would be huge. Although the difference was greater for those musicians who began musical training with stringed instruments as children, "even if you take up stringed instruments at forty," Taub commented, " you still get brain reorganization."

What a waste it would be to lose years of beneficial knowledge! This is even more motivation to help new guitarists on their journey. Let me wish you all success in this new experience. Should you turn out to be the next Jimi Hendrix, Eric Clapton, Jimmy Page, or Eddie Van Halen, bravo! I wish you all the best. Go out there, and blaze more trails. There's always room for another guitar virtuoso. I'd love to hear about it.

Choosing an Axe and Accessories

The guitar is sometimes referred to as an "axe." The term was coined long before there were actually guitars shaped like axes right out of antiquity. When first starting out, choosing the right guitar isn't as difficult as you might imagine. Walking into guitar showrooms can be a little overwhelming, though, with their plethora of brands and model styles, especially the first time. Don't let this intimidate you. First, ask yourself a few simple questions. Are you interested in an acoustic or an electric? Here are the pros and cons of both.

I will begin with the acoustic hollow body, which can be electrified. The acoustic is somewhat more difficult to handle and play, with its larger body, heavier-gauge steel strings, and higher action. Spanish and classical guitars have nylon strings, for a softer, mellower sound, and they are easier on the fingertips. Incidentally, the term "action" refers to the height of the strings off the fingerboard. New guitars are usually strung slightly higher. Until the frets have been broken in. String height is then set where you play the most on the fretboard. The advantage of starting out on an acoustic is that you don't need an amplifier. They can be amplified with a microphone or an attachable pickup and an amplifier. Acoustic guitars can be played anywhere, without the use of electricity. A good acoustic guitar can cost as much or even more than an electric guitar. If your heart is set on an acoustic, be aware that they are a little more difficult to learn on. I would recommend an electric guitar when first starting out. There are also semi-acoustic guitars, played with or without amplification. I never liked the sound quality of those without amplification.

My all-time favorite guitar is the electric. These have thinner bodies and necks and lighter-gauge strings with better action up the fretboard, but they need amplification. The electric's thinner body makes it easier to hold while playing. It is possible to hear an electric guitar without an amplifier, but it has limited sound projection and no sound quality.

Bottom line, simple economics may dictate your choice. Remember what is important. Is the guitar easy to play and have good sound quality? Does everything work on the guitar? Appearance isn't important to start with, but the price tag is. Keep your investment down, for a faster resale should you decide not to continue. If the guitar is inexpensive, you can pass it along or use it for decoration.

This section is dedicated to the bass guitar. What is your motivation for playing the bass? Many times, I've encountered people wanting to play the bass instead of the six-string, presuming that it would simpler to learn and easy to play. They would exclaim, "But it has only four strings!" I would retort, "There are five and six-string bass guitars too." As to the bass guitar's supposed easiness, nothing is father from the truth. For one thing, bass strings are a lot thicker than those on a six-string, making it harder to manipulate. You will still need to learn the same scales, as well as bass chords and other aspects of playing. I compare bass to drums: both carry the beat, but neither affords the music produced as with the six-string guitar. Rarely, if ever, will you find anyone singing along with a bass without the accompaniment of other, full-range instruments. Bass guitar scales are in the lower octaves but are the same notes and patterns as the six-string. You can always switch over to the bass after learning on the six-string. You'll only need to adjust to the heavier strings and fret and string spacing. Why not have the best of both guitar worlds? Remember, it will take far more effort to learn on those huge, piano-like strings. Believe me, I'm not berating bass guitarists. I use to play bass in a band. It is often said that a proficient bassist is actually better than a lead guitarist. That is because of their ability to manipulate the bass strings as well as the lead guitarist plays. If you want an easy instrument to learn, to look cool playing in a band, to be popular with the ladies, to make money without working, or to party all the time, forget about it. Most bass players play six-string guitar too. Keep all these points in mind when deciding what guitar to play.

Here is the lowdown on famous brand names versus lesser-known brands. For obvious reasons, I will refrain from mentioning individual company names. Those of you who have been on the scene for a while will be able to guess. I was in the market for an acoustic guitar. The one I had my eye on was a top brand name costing over five hundred dollars. This was back in 1972, so the equivalent today would be triple or more. This is a lot of money to shell out. I came across an exact copy while checking out other brands. This acoustic was made by a Japanese company new to producing guitars. It was half the cost, but people back then were dubious about foreign products—and with good reason, I might add. Keeping an open mind, I decided to make a comparison by closely examining the construction, sound quality, and types of wood used. There was absolutely no difference at all, other than the company names. As you might have guessed already, I bought the $250 acoustic. Foreign products can be equal to or superior to those from the United States. As the old saying goes, never judge a book by its cover. When considering the different brands, make this the rule. Pay close attention by keeping your eyes and ears wide open. Making the right choices saves a lot of expense.

Let's review the criteria. Shop around for price, and notice how the guitar plays and sounds. Is it constructed well? Remember, price is more important when shopping for that first guitar. When going to guitar stores, remember that it is a cutthroat business. Use this to your advantage by using one store against another. I personally use a guitar catalog that offers the lowest prices on instruments and accessories. Also look around at the various other avenues: garage, yard, or estate sales; Web sites like eBay; various newspapers; and your grapevine. I purchased my first guitar from a department store. It was not easy to play; however, the sound quality was good. As I was a beginning guitar player, it served me well.

If you become a serious guitarist and decide that it is time for a new guitar, there are other points to take into consideration. We will only touch on the important ones. Buying guitars and equipment can be almost as confusing as purchasing a car. In these times, there are just so many options to consider. Fortunately, most salespeople will be happy to fill you in. By the way, don't feel obligated to buy just because they assisted you. While inquiring, you will find legitimate features, while other options are unnecessary embellishments. I will cover just the important ones, leaving the frills to those pesky salespeople.

The first thing to consider is what type of music interests you. If it is of only one type, there are guitars specifically designed to accommodate that type of music. For instance, if the music is classical, folk, or flamenco, there are various acoustics or electric acoustics available. Then there are the jazz guitars; some have semi-hollow bodies, and others are solid-body guitars. This applies to bass guitars too. The twelve-string guitar is used in many genres, like blues, country, folk, and rock. The electric solid-body guitar, with its amplification, is suited to screaming single notes and distorted power chords in the typical rock-and-roll style. Once you decide on your musical niche, you might also consider a guitar that fits with your body type and that you feel comfortable playing.

Examine the many types of guitar finishes; some of them are practical, while others are not. Stay away from guitars with cracks of any size anywhere on the guitar. Stains and natural oil finishes are beautiful but not practical. These offer little surface protection for the wood. I had a natural finish put on my 1972 SG Gibson, and though it's beautiful, I now have to be extremely careful not to mar the wood. Better are lacquer and enamel coating, which protect the wood.

Guitars come in many shapes and sizes that are exotic and alluring. Ask yourself: is it really practical? Or is it all show and no go? When you can afford only one all-around good guitar, practicality takes precedence every time. My preference is for the shape reminiscent of the female form. You will find its shape comfortable against your body while standing, and it is contoured to your lap when sitting. Next, look at the construction of the guitar. This includes the woods used, plus hardware and electronic components like bridges, fingerboard, frets, tuning pegs, volume/tone pots, toggles, pickups, and input jack. Use the strings to check the neck by looking down the fretboard and making sure it is straight. The strings should be played all the way up the neck without a buzzing or rattling or a dead-sounding note. Always play the guitar to check it out. If you are new to the guitar, ask the seller to play it, or bring a friend to play it for you. Give a thorough examination not just to used guitars, but also to new guitars. Good craftsmanship always reveals quality. If it is not apparent, take a pass on that guitar. Defects do happen, even with the best of companies. Should you find that it is tolerable, you can usually get a good discount on the price.

There are major brand names, which is usually reflected in the pricing. Still, giving these guitars a good, close examination can reveal how inexpensively some parts are manufactured. Never be influenced by just the company name. Another old saying is, "You get what you pay for." In the present time, this simply is no longer true.

Most of the above also applies to amplifiers and accessories. Always be on the lookout for those discounted prices; some sales yield good savings. Various reasons can prompt sales, like overstocking, grand openings, and discontinued or slightly damaged products. A good rule of thumb is to always make comparisons with other brands. Compare product features, pricing, and warranties, and remember to try out the products at the store first. Better brands usually hold up under scrutiny and will have better guarantees.

Let's talk about amplifiers, better known as amps. Amps come in two different versions. With a combination amplifier (called a combo amp), the amp and speakers, horns, and tweeters all come together as one unit in one cabinet. The other option is to get an amplifier head with independent speaker cabinets, so you can build a system. Amps come in various wattages, starting at ten watts; the higher wattages give more output. The speakers range from five to fifteen inches, or even larger with PA systems, and can include tweeters or horns. Conventional six-string amplifiers generally use twelve-inch speakers and even ten-inch speakers, while keyboard players use fifteen-inch speakers or a combination of different sizes. Bassists use fifteen-inch speakers to produce low-frequency sounds. The six-string guitarist has been known to incorporate ten-inch, twelve-inch, and even fifteen-inch speakers, tweeters, and horns.

Then there are stereo amplifiers. Here is my first experience purchasing one. My synthesizer manual recommended using a stereo amp. The company that made the synthesizer suggested using a stereo keyboard combination amp to produce the best sound quality.

After hearing about this fantastic amp, I bought into it—hook, line, and sinker. Talk about being gullible! According to the stereo amp's manual, in order to achieve "true stereo sound," there had to be at least eight feet of separation. I should have known better, because this principle applies to home stereo systems. So in order to achieve stereo, I had to buy another amp or speaker cabinet. Most keyboard stereo amps come with a fifteen-inch speaker. With the addition of a six-string guitar amp equipped with two twelve's, sound quality was incredible. In the end, it was the best of both worlds, with maximum bass-to-treble range. I believe this is the reason why some players incorporate the use of twelve and fifteen-inch speakers, tweeters, and horns.

Here's a little common sense to remember. Turn off all of the equipment before unplugging or plugging in the guitar cord, cable, or electrical plug. Always pull cables, cords, and plugs using the ends, which are made for that purpose. You get a lot more life out of these accessories that way, and that makes it worth the little extra effort. This applies to all electronic equipment. Never place liquids such as beverages or cleaners on or near amplifiers or guitars. Apply cleaners sparingly, using a dry cloth. Keep both amps and guitars away from heat sources such as radiators, stoves, heaters, heat vents, computers, or other amplifiers. Excessive heat will cause amps to overheat and guitar finishes to crack and can even warp the neck. Also keep belt buckles, cufflinks, etc., away from the finish. I've seen some nasty gouges in the finish and on backs of guitars.

Let's move on to smaller accessories, starting with strings and the various sets. The gauge of the first string determines the name of the set. Electric guitars, and some acoustic ones, come with steel strings. Traditionally, electric guitars start with nine- or ten-gauge sets and acoustics with twelve- or thirteen-gauge sets. Acoustics produce more resonance with heavier-gauge sets. Some acoustics use nylon strings; it depends on what type it is. Never use steel strings on a nylon stringed acoustic! There are many types of set sizes. "Heavy-bottom" sets start out with the traditional nine-gauge, for example, but the rest of the strings become progressively larger than that of a regular set. I prefer a set starting out with a ten-gauge, because the strings offer a richer sound but are still easy to play, falling somewhere in between regular and heavy-bottom strings. I recommend staying with the standard-size sets until becoming a proficient player. After that point, you will be able to make an intelligent assessment by experimentation.

Always replace strings one at a time by loosening each one, not cutting them off, as this could cause the neck to warp. The neck needs the counter-force of the strings to keep it straight. It is by far better to leave on the old strings than to remove them and leave them off, as this too will allow the neck to warp. After replacing all of the strings, you should stretch them by using your fingers to pull each string away from the fretboard several times. Then tune each string as you go along. Here is an order that you can use for tuning. Tune the sixth string first, next go to the first, then the fifth, second, fourth, and finally the third. There is also a tool you can buy for stretching strings. If you don't stretch new strings, you will have to keep retuning while trying to play until the string stretches out. New strings will sometimes rattle or buzz for a short time after changing them, but only from the guitar itself. This sound shouldn't be heard through the amp or after the strings start to break in, and it may not be heard at all, depending on the individual guitar. It's a good practice to always check and see if the guitar is in tune before playing, and intermittently in between songs, or even more when recording. Replacing the strings brings new life to a guitar. This can be done every two to four weeks or longer, depending on how much you play. Here's a word of caution: new strings wrapped in a circle pose a potential hazard to you and others around you, including pets, as the strings spring out when opened. Little children and pets have a tendency to want to play with the strings, so keep them out of reach, and throw the old ones away immediately. This will help to prevent mishaps.

The plectrum, commonly known as the flat pick, was originally made from tortoiseshell, until the advent of plastic. There are many types of picks, including thumb picks and finger picks and other odd assortments. I have patented a few unusual ones called Guitar Sweeps. Most commonly used are the flat picks in the shape of a triangle with slightly rounded edges; these come in various sizes and thicknesses. In the beginning, I used thin picks, but these broke too often, and I ended up switching to medium picks. Picks, like strings, may take some getting used to. To achieve a sound with a punchy attack, a bassist will use a thick pick instead of fingertips.

Cords have come a long way and range from low to high in price. The synthesizer uses a cable. This is a case in which spending more is actually better. Some come with a lifetime warranty and are very dependable but will cost accordingly. You'll need to pay attention when buying a cord, as jacks come with two different ends. One is a straight end, and the other has a ninety-degree angle to accommodate the different inputs. Check with the store for one you need.

The guitar case is never given enough consideration, in my opinion. This is an essential accessory. The better the guitar, the better the case should be. If it's your first, inexpensive guitar, you'll want to keep down the expense down. A simple gig bag will do. When finally making that big investment on an excellent guitar, by all means, don't skimp on the cost of its case. A good case is worth every penny spent on it for the protection it offers. This is especially true if you travel and other people will be handling it, like the brutal airlines.

Let's move on to effects. I have spent numerous hours trying out a myriad of these devices. The old standards are; reverb, echo, distortion, wah-wah pedal, harmonizer, octave divider, chorus, arpeggiator, and tremolo. Companies are always trying to come up with new product lines. In my opinion, most aren't worth the money, especially when they first come out. Occasionally something comes out that is kind of interesting; however, the investment is debatable. I have spent hours searching for unique sounds to build up my arsenal of effects for a space music project, only to find just two boxes. Both had multiple effects, but I only found two cool settings on each. It seemed hardly worth all the money I put out, but I was desperate for any new sounds. Ordinarily I would have passed on both.

When contemplating new products, keep in mind that the prices will inevitably come down with time.

Usually the longer you can hold out, the better the savings. Be aware of the sales technique called a "gimmick." This means a trick or device to attract attention or publicity. On the surface, a gimmick looks good, but you need to ask yourself if it is really what it appears to be. The salesperson will say, "Technology—isn't it great?" Just remember, all that glitters is not gold. Use discretion while that pretty-colored, shiny new gizmo is being dangled in front of you. Play every setting instead of believing what you're being told. There are some inept salespeople out there who are just trying to make a sale. Keep in mind that if it looks too good to be true, maybe it is.

Here's a funny little Christmas story about my first super guitar. It was the month before Christmas 1964, and I was anticipating what might be under the tree. I had hoped the effort I'd put forth had proved my sincerity about playing and would bring a quality guitar. Saving enough money at fourteen to get a decent guitar would take a long time, even for a good used one.

Santa knew what was on my list, but gifts were always kept secret. I knew that my family was impressed with my progress, but even back then, guitars were expensive. There was a hint in the air, which gave me hope.

It was almost impossible to sleep on Christmas Eve. I arose early and anxiously waited for the family to gather. There were no gifts under the tree with my name, other than a big, flat, oblong box, which added to the excitement. My anticipation was off the scale. At last the family was gathered around the tree with cameras in hand, and it was my turn to open my gift. When I opened the box, my eyes popped out of my head. I couldn't believe what I saw. There it sat in front of me, with its red metal-flake finish and not one, but four pickups, accommodated by all kinds of knobs and switches—the super guitar! *Wow!* Back then; even rock stars didn't have guitars like that. Could this be really be happening to me? I was elated. How could my family afford this?

Moments later, I ran off into my room to check this bad boy out. Tuned up and ready to go, I twisted knobs, flipped switches, and changed pickup combinations without success. I wasn't able to get a good, clean, crisp sound out of it. Even my department store model could do that.

Dismayed, I returned it to the folks and told them about its horrible sound quality. They perceived this as being ungrateful. This was to be the first Christmas I wouldn't receive a gift. They returned it. In hindsight, I realize that they had no conception about guitars and felt insulted by my attitude. Everyone was disappointed that year.

This story does have a happy ending. In spite of this, I still kept up with improving my guitar skills. Five months later, on my fifteenth birthday, they bought me a great used name-brand guitar. It might not have been the model I wanted, but it played well and sounded great. Later, I got a part-time job and saved up enough money to get the guitar I wanted.

Practice, Patience, Perseverance, Precision — How, When, and Where

There are many philosophies on how to practice and learn, and I tend to disagree with most of them. For instance, I don't believe half-hour practice sessions are of much benefit when first starting out. I have used my method with past and present students to a great degree of success.

Let's assume you are starting off from square one, and we'll go into full detail. If you have already been playing for a while, just glance over parts of this. Again, this book is not about learning music theory or technical aspects like fingering or strumming techniques.

Let's start out with how and when to practice. When starting out, practicing should be in short bursts. For beginners, this will be anywhere from thirty seconds to a minute or so. After a week or so, start to gradually increase the time to a few minutes and then more. How much time you add is based on how much your abilities have improved. It is better to start with shorter time frames. Stay focused, and come back later, one or even two more times throughout the day. Using this method will expedite the learning process. If you want to alleviate boredom, alternate between chords and scales. As you become more accomplished, throw in songs you've learned that you enjoy. Remember, it's important to concentrate at all times when practicing. Mindless practice will only stretch out the learning process. Like reading, if you don't concentrate, you will find yourself having to reread.

Here are some exercises you can do without much thought. These are simple fretboard hand exercises. Squeeze a small, soft rubber ball using the fingertips only, if you have larger hands, an *old* racquetball will do. This builds up the hand and finger muscles. Holding up the palm of your hand in front of you, spread open your fingers, hold for five seconds, and then relax. Do this five to ten times. This is one set. Repeat three times. This finger-stretching exercise will help with hard-to-reach chords and notes.

For faster dexterity, use these next two exercises. Hold open your fretboard hand, and touch each individual fingertip to your thumb, starting with your index finger and continuing to the pinky and back. Do this ten to twenty times. A similar but harder exercise is to open your fretboard hand and then bring the index and ring fingertips as close to the palm as possible. Alternate with the middle and pinky fingers, and do this ten to twenty times. At first this takes full concentration, but eventually it can be done without much effort or thought. These exercises are convenient, because you don't need a guitar.

These exercises build dexterity, and once mastered, they can be practiced perfunctorily. Doing dexterity exercises and practicing scales can be used as a warm-up procedure.

Here is another helpful tip. If you find yourself becoming bored or discouraged, put down the guitar and return a little later. As you become more proficient at executing what you have practiced, it will almost seem magical, motivating you to move forward. Always practice slowly and with precision. Never practice fast. Speed comes naturally after the ability is gained through precision practicing. No one wants a sloppy guitarist; play tasty licks, not hasty notes, by learning your chops right. "Chops" is a word used to mean guitar licks or riffs—a succession of notes. Whenever learning new things, no matter what they are, give it time, to avoid exasperation. It is also impractical to expect to immediately play as well as your teacher. If you consider how long it took the teacher to learn, it would be a little disconcerting if students were able to immediately play just as well. Of course, on rare occasions, there are exceptional students. I have seen them, and I was amazed to the point of being a little envious. I have had the pleasure of teaching one of them, but it is by far not the norm. Remember, for the rest of us, it is the four P's: practice with patience, perseverance, and precision.

Anxiety is to be avoided while practicing or performing. This causes the muscles to contract and become tense. The guitarist needs relaxed arms, hands, and fingers for fluency. When your muscles tense up, it won't be too much longer before you cramp and then have to stop. Anxiety happens when you are trying too hard, or it can be in the form of stage fright. If this starts to occur, take a minute to calm down. I use a deep breathing technique that helps. Try to find a secluded quit place to sit. Now take five to ten slow, deep breaths; you should see your stomach extend forward. If you hear yourself breathing, slow down and start over. This technique relaxes the whole body and can be used in any stressful situation.

Here are some tips for the fingertips. Never practice or play with wet hands. The longer the hands are submerged in water, the longer it will take before they are completely dry. So when swimming, showering, or even sweating for a long time, it takes longer for the hands to dry out than if only doing dishes for a few minutes. It would be a shame to lose those hard-earned calluses. The same is true for overdoing it by playing or practicing too long. The fingertips will develop blisters, like burn blisters. This would put you right back to the start. You'll have to wait to heal and build new calluses. If you are starting out, it will take a few weeks to form strong calluses. Stop after the fingertips hurt and become red. Of course you will have to endure some pain in the beginning—no pain, no gain—but do it in moderation. This is another reason to begin with very short practice sessions.

Avoid infections caused by cuts or biting fingernails or tips. The human mouth is loaded with germs. Biting your nails or fingertips will make the broken skin susceptible to infection. Use a pumice stone to remove any excessive hardened skin or callus. Use a nail file instead of nail clippers. Keep a nail file on hand inside your guitar case.

On the fingerboard hand, keep nails just below the tips; this lends support to the fingertips for pressing down on the strings. If you fingerpick, keep your nails slightly longer; hanging over the tips about an eighth to a quarter inch on the picking hand, whatever is your preference. If using fingerpicks, keep the nails on your picking hand the same length as those on the fingerboard hand. When filing your nails, slightly file around the edges; going too far will injure the fingertips, make them sore, and lead to infection. Keep the area under your fingernails clean. If you get a sliver under your nail, force antibiotic ointment under the nail every day until the nail grows, pushing out the sliver; this will also help with the soreness. It is also a good idea to keep the fretboard clean by wiping it down after playing. The hands are a main focal point on the guitarist and draw the attention of the audience.

Where we practice holds importance too. As discussed earlier, bad choices affect others. Be concerned about others—especially family, friends, roommates, and neighbors—when you practice. Aggravating people can bring unnecessary problems, like the police, or the loss of potential future customers. Find a place somewhere where you won't be disturbing others, one that is quiet so you won't be distracted. Here's some sound advice (pun intended): when learning, practicing, playing, or writing a new piece, use a practice amp or recording device with a headphone input. This is an advantage of the electric guitar. Practice silently; after all, you wouldn't want someone driving you crazy with repetitive sound. When using headphones, keep the volume down to a reasonable level, or you will go deaf; that is, unless you believe you are able to pull off what Ludwig von Beethoven did.

If the band you are in needs a place to practice, rent a rehearsal room or space where the band won't bother anyone. A garage, barn, warehouse, or basement can be an option when on a tight budget.

Here are some avenues to which to market your experience, talent, and music: selling guitars and equipment; teaching; playing clubs, bars, social gatherings, parties, dances, park district gatherings, or malls; and—you street musicians—open that guitar case for cash.

Another possibility is producing movie soundtracks or music for computer games. Companies and corporations buy music for commercials and TV shows. With a little imagination, you can come up with some ideas to market your talent, like my writing this book.

The Guitarist's Lifestyle

My mother was a big music enthusiast who sang like a songbird and played the keyboard. I was born in 1951, when Mom was sixteen years old. As a young child, I remember the neighborhood teenage girls coming over to hang out and play the latest rock-and-roll 45 RPM records. During that time, I was also exposed to my grandparents' generation of music. At every family gathering, Grandpa would bring out his banjo, and Grandma would be on the organ, and they would sing their generation's songs. Listening to both generations of popular music instilled a strong interest in music and lent to my diverse musical background. At home, our record player and radios were in constant use. Even when we went out to eat, the restaurant and burger-joint jukeboxes were always on, playing the hits. I was predisposed to music before I could talk or walk. When I was sick at night, Mom would play soothing music like Johnny Mathis to lull me asleep. Looking back, my becoming a musician was set in motion long before that fateful day when I first picked up the guitar.

Music has held me captive since the dawn of rock and roll. The songs of that period later became part of my repertoire as a new guitarist. As a young boy, my first idol was Elvis Presley. I loved all of his music and movies. When I was a preteen, there was an explosion of new teen idols like Chuck Berry, Jerry Lee Lewis, Mitch Rider and the Detroit Wheels, the Beach Boys, and Jan and Dean, to name but a few.

In 1964, I was thirteen at the beginning of the British invasion. My idols then were bands like the Beatles, the Who, and the Rolling Stones. We had our great bands too in the United States, like the Doors, Iron Butterfly, Steppenwolf, the Strawberry Alarm Clock, and the Byrds. I was smitten by all of them. The songs of all of these great artists added to my repertoire throughout the years.

That generation of musicians not only changed music but also changed lives, and mine in particular. Their music and lyrics influenced a whole generation, and by observation of today's youth, I've determined that they still do. Big rock artists held so much influence, in fact, that even the authorities and politicians were well aware of them. In yet another way, this is still felt in almost every household across America; you can tell by the guitar sitting in the corner somewhere in the house. Changed were the ideals, beliefs, directions, ambitions, and even dress of that generation and the generations after it. This was not only in the individual and our nation; eventually it went out to the world. Should you have an interest in taking guitar to a professional level, please read on. If not, you may skip over the rest of this chapter.

When you're thirteen, you don't have a clue about what lifestyle changes come about after you've decided to become a serious guitarist. At first the changes are subtle, like taking care of your hands or saving enough allowance for strings and picks. Then it starts to progress to new levels. You'll find yourself wanting new or better equipment, and now you will need to get a part-time job. To play professionally, you'll need more than one type of guitar, and if you sing, you will also need a microphone and another amp. Guitar playing can just as easily stay a hobby, or new goals can keep spiraling forward, as they did for me. Quite frankly, even as a hobby, it needs a certain level of commitment.

Hollywood can make the musician's lifestyle look glamorous. The truth is that there is more than meets the eye. As you know, there will be the same considerations about sports activities or what kinds of jobs to take while not working as guitarist. Band and personal practice will take up a lot of time, and if you write, that takes even more time. This is a lot of work, but if you love your job, it's not really work, right? If you're still going to school, the same things apply.

Look closely at a guitarist's physique, and you'll notice that one shoulder is lower. This comes from years of playing, particularly when starting at a young age. As an entertainer at gatherings, you work instead of partying. Don't assume that being at the festivities makes it okay to party too, unless your performance is over. There is something to be said about the old adage of not mixing business with pleasure; that is, if you're really serious about becoming successful.

Being on the road puts on a lot of wear and tear, even when maintaining a business atmosphere. On the surface, it sounds great. You get to hang out with your band members, meet cool people, and travel while seeing new places. But traveling artists hardly get to be at home, and this is certainly not conducive to a family lifestyle. Day in and day out, musicians live out of their suitcases and in hotel rooms. There are, however, a few artists that do manage by taking their families on the road, but they will be the first ones to tell you how incredibly difficult it is for the whole family. Most artists' give up the regular lifestyle in pursuit of their craft, by placing it above marriage, children, and a home or at the least, they put these things off until later in their career.

On the darker side of the business, there are the drugs and alcohol that took the lives of great artists like Jim Morrison, Janis Joplin, and Jimi Hendrix, to name but a few. In addition are the STDs, one of which took the life of Queen's Freddie Mercury. Included in this menagerie of mayhem are the headaches better known as head-trips. These include being ripped off by managers, agents, promoters, publishers, or record companies and inner disputes among band members. Then there is the media side, which can lead to being misunderstood or sued, or even criminal charges. Watch out for the vamps that want to suck the life out of you with their ulterior motives, like fair-weather friends or women that only want marriage to rich and famous men. It can be a lonely life on top, as you're in a class by itself. Other creative artists encounter this too. Included are songwriters, singers, actors, artists, models, producers, directors, and managers of big acts. You need a strong constitution, and you need to tread carefully when you have star status. This is the reason why a lot of artists and bands don't last that long. This happened to the Beatles, causing the breakup that shook and saddened millions of fans. As a young guitarist, I used to wonder what it meant when they said, "Great artists are born through suffering and anguish"; now it's no longer a mystery.

I'm not trying to paint a bleak picture here to scare you off, but in all fairness to you, these are cold, hard facts that you need to know. Again, if you're only playing for self-gratification or fun, friends, and family, you needn't concern yourself.

You can't imagine how easy it is to get caught up in all of this, but it happens all the time. When your ability to play the guitar exceeds all expectations, you'll start thinking, "Why not go for it?" How can you lose with all this talent? Unfortunately, it's not how much talent you possess or how excellent you are at playing, writing, or singing. It's sad but true that most of the time, unless you're extremely lucky, this isn't enough. You will still need financial backing, excellent and trustworthy people behind you, great music connections, and a whole lot of luck to become successful. Nowadays, record companies like a CD to be already recorded and want the artist or band to have a strong following. They might even ask for up-front capital for the promotions. Fortunately, there are now home recording units that can do the job on a professional level; of course, you'll need to engineer it.

Back in the day, it was possible to get a break on the merit of talent, but that's not the case anymore. Recording technology can make anyone sound great. Add this to a well-written commercial song—sometimes not even that—and bam, you could have a hit song. Sometimes all that is needed now is good promotions pumping up an image, and bam, there's a new celebrity. The formula has been repeated time and time again with great success. The original test took place back in the mid sixties with a group called the Monkees, which was put together by producers.

Remember, the music business is no different than any other business; it's all about making money. Realize that in essence, you are just another product. This sounds cold, but when you aren't commercially viable anymore, there's rarely a second chance. This also applies to all the other types of artists out there. No matter what your art is, it must produce a profit; otherwise, to the business world, it's useless. This is no different than if you work for a company. If they feel that your productivity is not up to their standards, you will be replaced.

No one could anticipate how a simple thing like learning to play the guitar could change his or her life. In retrospect, I never realized that when I decided to make music my ambition in life, everything would change. Compare this to a road trip without a destination, when one arbitrary turn changes everything, leaving your destination unknown until you arrive. My life as a guitarist came with great times and hardships that I will always remember, but you'll find that everything in life really is a trade-off. What comes to mind is an old ancient Chinese proverb: "Joy can't be known without sorrow." Getting married and having children and a house were never my ambition. I choose not to, in favor of less entanglement. I attribute this more to my observations of family and friends growing up, so I never missed not engaging in it.

I grew up in the Midwest, in a suburb twenty miles west of Chicago. In high school, I was a big fish in a little pond. My reputation preceded me. Musicians from neighboring high schools would come to recruit me. While living in Los Angeles, I attended a movie production business meeting as a guest of a good friend and actor named Tony. A writer who had been imported from Chicago came into the meeting, and I was the last in line to be introduced. I could see the look of excitement growing in his eyes as he approached, and I wondered what was up. He spewed out the words, " Oh, my god—it's Tim Sarno!" Everyone turned, giving me a second look, as if to say, *Who is this guy, anyway?* I was taken aback and embarrassed. Well, it turned out that he had gone to the same high school as I did. He was a couple of years younger and had always wanted to ask me for guitar lessons but was too shy. It's a small, small world after all.

I have always heard if a person is really serious about a music career, he needs to "go west, young man"—for this was where to find your fame and fortune. So one day, I saved up a little money, sold most of my things, and headed west. I moved to Santa Monica, California, and spent over two decades there without much luck. Oh, I met all kinds of rich and famous people and even worked for Arnold Schwarzenegger. I could give you quite an impressive list, but it was all to no avail.

You see, in Chicago, I was a big fish in a little pond, but in Los Angeles, I was swallowed up in a big sea full of talented fish. Some lessons are learned the hard way. On the other hand, should you ponder becoming serious about music, please don't let this sway you, as things could turn out very differently. Even if you venture forth and run into some difficulties, remember that anything worth having comes with a price. I've never regretted one minute of my life. If you decide to perform music and have a family too, just be aware that it's a juggling act and you'll have to be good at maintaining a balance.

Perhaps your ambition is only to make a decent living as a guitarist. This will improve the opportunity to live a more normal life with a family. Of course, the same bad elements that ensnare musicians are still pervasive, and it still comes down to individual choices. Making wise decisions will make all the difference in the world. Music can offer a lucrative career if you work hard and don't get caught up in the negative aspects. It's great to be dedicated, but here are some words of advice. Be realistic, and don't set your standards too high. Stay away from delusions of grandeur. Setting your goals too high can lead to extreme disappointment, depression, or even worse. If you're realistic and aware of the pitfalls, you can avoid many problems. This is the key to a happy and successful life.

For the serious guitarist, here are some other points to take into consideration. Careful thought should be put into participation in hard contact sports like football, karate, boxing, wrestling, and hockey; these aren't advisable. There are other, safer sports you can play instead. Added to this are the ridiculous macho schoolboy games like arm wrestling, punching, and slapping wet fingers against each other's arms to achieve welt marks. It may seem like innocent fun, but the consequences could be devastating. Think about the action before acting out. You won't be able to participate or play with a sprain or worse, broken bones. Have consideration for others, like band members or people that you are suppose to entertain. I must be careful when opening heavy doors with my strumming hand. If I push the door open with my palm and fingers pointing upward, it is a guaranteed sprained wrist. This has been a problem for me ever since learning to play guitar. A guitarist needs a supple wrist for strumming, but this makes you susceptible to wrist sprain.

As a boy, I loved to whittle wood. When I became older, this hobby expanded to woodcarving. If there is a hobby you absolutely love and don't want to give up, make it a point to read up on it, learning the right and safe way. Some of the first rules I learned about using a knife were always to cut away from the body and never to take your eyes off the knife while it is in use. I would advise another hobby, because one false move, and your guitar playing could be over.

Playing guitar goes along with the fact that I love working with my hands. Not being able to afford college and realizing how hard it is to make money with music, I decided to pursue the trades. I ended up as a maintenance worker or handyman, which I would not recommend for a guitar player. I did pay close attention while working, but I still encountered a few close calls. Like with carving, I derived a feeling of accomplishment upon completing a successful repair job. If you find yourself in a similar situation, I acquiesce.

Being big for my age, I passed for sixteen and landed a job at a local factory as a spot welder. I quickly made enough money to purchase another amplifier but kept the job to buy others things, such as accessories and records. One day, I decided not to go in, and my best friend, Loui, took my place on a new job detail. I was to be trained to run a punch press. When I didn't show up, they used Loui instead. The punch press malfunctioned, causing him the loss of the use of his left index finger. That would have ended my guitar playing. Fortunately, it just wasn't in the cards for me. Somehow, I've always felt responsible for the mishap, even though it wasn't my fault. Needless to say, I quit that job the very next day.

Deciding on a Teacher

My fascination with stringed instruments began as a little boy with my stepfather's Hawaiian (steel) guitar, which he kept in his closet. As I recall, he rarely brought it out to play, if ever, but I knew it was in there. I could never resist the urge to sneak into the closet and pluck on those strings. Over and over, I would sneak in the closet to strum and pluck the strings so I could listen to the wonderful sounds it produced. I often wondered how he could ignore his instrument. It would have driven me crazy, like it does now when I don't play for a while.

Grandfather had a banjo and a ukulele in his closet. When he wasn't around, I'd secretly slip off into the attic and pretend to play them both, though these didn't hold my interest nearly as much as that steel guitar. I never really knew if either of them would have minded, but I was too afraid to ask. I kind of suspected that they might say no, and I didn't want to take that chance. Even as a young child, I knew that I was probably being a bad boy, but certainly it seemed worth the risk to play. As you know, I was given that ukulele, but by that time, my mind was set on the guitar. Oddly enough, to this day, I've never had the interest in learning steel guitar, probably because the slide used on other guitars is very similar. I guess I only had eyes—or should I say ears?—for guitar.

After what seemed like forever to get my first guitar, how would I learn to play? My family and I couldn't afford lessons. So I went to my grandfather, but he informed me that banjo was different from guitar and said he couldn't help me there. But after I had been playing for a while, he did teach me the secrets of playing by ear, something he could do quite well. In this case, the similarities between banjo and guitar made this possible. This gave me a huge advantage over other guitar players, as I was able to pick up lead notes and chords simply by listening to records and radio.

I have always found it somewhat strange that trained guitarists, like classical players, find it difficult to pick up rock and roll. Other rockers I've spoken with have encountered the same. Give them the sheet music or show the song's structure, and they can play it all right, but the music lacks the subtle nuances of rock and roll. Maybe as they were still in high school, they were all too young and couldn't make the transition. I never had a clue as to why. But that always seemed to be the case every time I asked one of them to teach me how to play a rock and roll song. It was the same when I auditioned one of them for my band. I would try to show him how, but he just couldn't seem to grasp it. Needless to say, I didn't take lessons from any of them. This certainly wasn't the case with bands like Blood, Sweat & Tears or Chicago, who were all trained musicians. Though their music seemed a little too much on the technical side for my taste, I still liked a few of their songs.

It seemed that my luck was about to change. Mom told me she had spoken with an older second cousin who had agreed to give lessons. Wow, was I excited, not only because I had a teacher but also because he was in a rock-and-roll band. At last it was time to get down to learning some serious rock, man. Oh, yeah! Cousin Jimmy came over and gave me three lessons over a period of three weeks. At the end of the third week, he came over to check on my progress and, I thought, to give another lesson. He listened and then turned around and walked out to inform my mother of my lack of talent and ability. Okay, folks, before we go any farther here, you should know that this was Mom's favorite cousin and she had all the confidence in the world in his opinion, especially when it had came to music and rock and roll. Remember, he had been playing for quite a while and was in a rock band. So off to the garage it was for me, and "We don't want to hear it until—or if—you learn how to play." *He's got to be kidding. Three weeks?* I thought. *Could that possibly be enough time to make that evaluation?* Well, now I know that it isn't. Feeling put out and mad, I became determined to prove him wrong. So off I went into the garage and persisted. Some people just aren't cut out to be teachers.

Remembering what Grandpa said about playing by ear, I plodded along, listening to a couple of my favorite songs, "Day Tripper" by the Beatles and "Satisfaction" by the Rolling Stones, and somehow I managed to learn them on my own. I was so proud of myself as I played them to my surprised family. Mom suggested that I go over to Cousin Jimmy's house to show him, so I did. He sat there with a surprised look on his face, but not for the reason I thought. He was amazed by the fact that I was playing the lead to "Day Tripper" with only my index finger. Sometimes I still do this for kicks, and it's still difficult to do. Still, I had proven my point by showing my potential to not only play but also to learn by ear. Jimmy watched me play the notes, and then he showed me how to use all of my fingers. That seemed to make it harder to play.

Then I showed him the open country chords I used in "Satisfaction" and "Day Tripper." He smiled again and said that in order to learn rock and roll, I needed to learn something called bar chords. He proceeded to show me how to play bar chords, and I was horrified. Surely he was just getting back at me by messing with my head. I didn't say a word and left, admittedly with a little attitude. The next day I went to the store and bought a book on advanced chords, and sure enough, there they were, right in front of my eyes. It looked like Jimmy was on the up and up after all. So back out to the garage I went, and I practiced for what seemed like an eternity, trying to get the fingering down along with those bar chords. He was right: both the fingering and the bar chords were essential to learn, particularly in order to play rock and roll. It's funny to see the expression on my students' faces whenever I show them the same things. They just look at me in disbelief.

It wasn't too much longer before I started my own band. Cousin Jimmy, hearing of this, wanted in, because his band had broken up. Unfortunately I had everybody I needed, so I suggested that we start another band with his remaining band members. We gave it a shot, but it just didn't work out. Jimmy didn't have a lot of patience, as you might have guessed from his teaching. I'm pretty sure about this too. Some time later, his younger brother, who was just a little younger than I was, approached me for lessons. I said yes, but I asked why he didn't ask his brother. After all, we lived on the opposite ends of town, and neither of us drove. His comment was that his big brother lacked the patience.

I went on playing for quite a while on my own. Then I met an older gentleman from the neighborhood. His name was Vaughn, and he was more into country music but liked some rock. He watched me play and mentioned that I was doing something called flat fingering and said that I had some other technical problems that needed sorting out. Vaughn said that I should take some lessons, unless I didn't mind playing like Neil Young. I told him that I happened to like Neil Young, and I asked what was wrong with his playing. He said, "Nothing, except that he plays lead on the flat parts of his fingers instead of his fingertips, and that limits your ability to articulate your notes." I asked if he would teach me, but he declined, saying that it wasn't his thing. He told me to stop by any time, and we could play together. I did stop over many times, and in spite of what he'd said, he did give me a lot of tips, which at the time seemed a little ironic. We became good friends for the next year or so, and then he passed away from cancer. It wasn't until then that I understood why he didn't want to teach. He never told me about it. I still took his advice and went to the local music store for lessons.

By then, I had a part-time job, so off I went to the local music store. I signed up, and here is how my first few lessons went. I was taken to a small cubicle, where an older gentleman sat waiting with a cigarette in one hand and a coffee cup in the other. The smoke in that little room was suffocating. I know what you're thinking: why didn't I say something? But you have to remember that this was back in the sixties, and it wasn't known for sure if it harmed you; besides, both of my parents smoked. The teacher shows me how to play the music for "Sparkling Stella (Twinkle, Twinkle, Little Star)," handed me the sheet music, and left. He came back twenty-five minutes later, listened to me butcher the song one time, and then told me to go home and practice a half-hour a day and to please pay at the front desk on my way out. I can still remember how I felt about going back. It reminded me of having to go back to the dentist's office. I gave up and never returned to that music store. Later I went to yet another music store and took a few more lessons. They had a young teacher who taught rock and roll, but the results were pretty much the same. I did learn a few more things that helped me along the way. Fortunately, as time went by, I came across other accomplished guitar players, who helped in refining my techniques.

All this is not to say that you shouldn't look for a good teacher. I teach, and I have been told that I'm quite efficient at it. I do, however, believe that it takes a certain type of personality and a lot of patience to be a proficient teacher. A lot of students lack patience; add an impatient teacher, and you have a recipe for disaster. It is also important to be encouraging yet honest. Even students can spot a phony. I have worked at a college and have had the opportunity to observe other teachers with their students looking bored out of their minds. In order to keep a student's attention, a teacher needs to have a little entertainer inside of him. This is part of my teaching technique, and it goes over well with my students and holds their attention. Sometimes even just smiling does the trick. Of course you don't want to go overboard, as this can encourage the wrong atmosphere. I've found this method is successful because it makes the lesson fun. As my students progress, we play together, which brings enjoyment to the lesson. This promotes the student's confidence, by showing them how good they can sound. This works on the principle that a good guitarist can make even a mediocre guitarist sound good.

I strongly believe that these are the qualities that a student should look for in a good teacher. It goes without saying that teachers should know music and the guitar inside out and backwards, like Jimi Hendrix.

Should you decide to teach yourself, here is some practical advice to remember. As a beginner, the basics, like how to hold the guitar and finger position on the fretboard, are very important. You must also learn the correct way to play chords and scales. Some of you will find playing the scales difficult, while for others, it will be the chords. Get yourself some books at the library or from the store. Practice the four P's. Watch music videos with guitar players that show their hands while playing. As I recall, Pink Floyd's *Pulse* and footage of Jimi Hendrix live at Woodstock focused on their hands, to name but a couple. Go to live concerts, and pay close attention to the guitarists' fingers. This will all help tremendously, and you'll enjoy it. If you're too young to go alone, get one or both of your parents to take you: trust me, they will enjoy it too.

You should also check around with friends and relatives for someone to teach you. Have them ask their brothers and sisters to look around for you. If you're a guy and you happen to run across a female teacher, don't discriminate, I've heard some hot female guitarists before. You are periodically still going to need to have someone check up on you, so you don't develop bad techniques. I can tell you firsthand, because this has happened to me. Having to learn how to play again, but using my fingertips, was a lot harder then if I had learned it right in the first place. It's true when they say that bad habits are hard to break.

Don't be confused by the different styles of guitar playing; use whichever works the best for you. Everyone's hands are slightly different, so what works for one person might not work for another. You can adopt a style that suits you or a combination of styles. It's inevitable that you'll develop your own style anyway. If you are going to be an entertainer, you can't be shy, so be bold and ask as many guitarists as possible. It's not rude to seek help from others. When I encounter problems, even to this day, as I did while recording, I turn and ask another guitarist for suggestions. If you find that you're having too much trouble on your own, then it would be prudent to get help, whether from a teacher or another guitarist.

We won't go into songwriting here, but I have one last story to tell. I took a songwriting class while I was living in Santa Monica. It was held at UCLA. I had been writing songs for over ten years when I saw the advertisement. I wanted to see if I was on the right track and decided to take the class. The teacher's credentials were very impressive, as he had written hit songs for many major artists like Presley, Sinatra, Manilow, Como, and Boone. Like most of the others in class, I was in awe. His confidence filled the classroom. He had a twenty-step method. As we went further along, my confidence grew, and toward the end, I realized that I hadn't really needed the class after all.

There was an older man in the back of the classroom that would always heckle the teacher. He looked scruffy and unkempt, and at first I thought he was just being a jerk. It was such an annoyance that several times the teacher had offered his money back to get him to leave. The man had flat-out refused, saying that he didn't want the money.

At the end the class, we had to write a song and play it for the class, which I promptly did. I was so excited about getting the teacher's opinion. I played it, and everyone in class liked the song. I thought that was a good sign, and anxiously I awaited the teacher's response. He told me the lyrics were prolific and who did I think I was, Stevie Wonder? That was the end of his critique, without even as much as a word about the melody. Once again, the man in the back spoke out in strong disagreement. It was then that I finally realized whom the arrogant one in this classroom really was.

It goes without saying that I've not had very good luck with music teachers. But it doesn't mean that you won't either. Again, even if learning on your own, periodically find someone that has been playing for at least a year or so, and have them check on your progress. Good luck.

The Magic in Music

Have you ever heard about the magic in music? Do you think this is something that only children believe in? What about the Pied Piper or the seductive music of Pan's flute? Okay, I know these were only allegories, but it's said that even stories like these hold some truth. Read on, because here is some really cool stuff that I'm sure you'll find intriguing.

Let's give music its due. We love to play that sweet, sweet music and have those listening feel our expression. After all, for the most part, this is what becoming a guitarist is all about. We all love music, and you'll find it all over the world. Music has long been the mystical art of producing sound waves that influence the state of mind, releasing emotions. Current research is revealing proof that music and sound can enhance or detract from a person's well-being. In the past twenty years, sound waves in various pitches and timings have been used to produce relaxation; this is part of what is known as biofeedback. This moves a person from the conscious (beta) state to a relaxed state of mind called the alpha state. Around the same time, it was also discovered by air traffic controllers that flashing lights put the controller into an entranced state of mind. Combining these ideas, a light and sound machine called an LS machine was invented. The LS machine uses light and sound concurrently with headphones and glasses that have LED lights. It was found that the combination could place subjects into the deeper states of consciousness called theta and delta. I have enjoyed the use of an LS machine for stress release and relaxation for over ten years. If you are interested in information about LS machines, go to Mind-Gear.com. If you're ordering, tell them I said hello.

Government research has found that producing sound waves at the right frequencies can be used as a form of weaponry. You have probably seen example of the effect sound has when a loud stereo moves speakers and other things on a shelf. We know that high-pitched sound can shatter a glass, but did you know it is also used to fuse together plastic tool handles? In the bible, it is said that trumpets brought down the walls of Jericho. Recently it was proven that this could very well have taken place. Other research has shown very low frequencies to be debilitating and disorienting to humans, and it can be used as non-lethal weaponry. Currently there is some speculation among scientists that sound could have been used to levitate the massive stone blocks used to build the pyramids in Egypt. Think of all the other amazing applications that will be discovered as research progresses.

Sound frequencies have been and are currently used in the medical field. In some cases, it has actually replaced surgery and pharmaceuticals. For instance, ultrasound is currently used in several medical applications, such as muscle spasms, kidney stone dispersal, and cataract removal. More recently, medical scientists applied a specific resonant frequency to excite the cancerous cells of a tumor, which vibrates the cells to the extent that they rupture, thus destroying the tumor. Scientists at Arizona State University have used vibrations to kill viruses. In India, Sanskrit scholars have initiated a research project, said to be the first of its kind, to treat various diseases through Vedic chants. What other applications will be discovered as medical research progresses?

I own an acoustic field generator, also known as an AFG. The AFG is composed of home stereo speakers, a CD or cassette player, and an amplifier. Also included are a tape or CD with various sound frequencies, which are then played through the speakers. The speakers are placed into cushions, which I lie upon to absorb sound into my whole body. My sound-wave bed is made into a pair of three by three-and-a-half-foot cushions for easy transport. Each cushion holds a twelve-inch woofer speaker. I have had mine for over ten years, and I love it. It's like a total body massage without the pressure and pain of a body massage. While on the bed, you can feel the waves transferring through you. There is also a residual effect that you can still feel for quite some time afterward. I'm optimistic about future prospects for helping people medically by natural, alternative means.

The first movies were called silent movies and weren't accompanied by soundtracks. Instead they had subtitles and were accompanied by a person playing a piano. They would play along with the movie, setting the mood by adding emphasis and ambience to the film. Filmmakers are very aware of this and utilize it to the max, with songs or orchestrations set to time limits of tenths of a second. Music is strategically positioned throughout the film to bring out our emotions at the right time and place. We experience many different emotions throughout a movie. A good soundtrack can bring out sadness, joy, fear, happiness, anxiety, excitement, horror, elation, and even pride. Light and sound, like the LS machine, were used in movies as far back as *Gone With the Wind* and are still used extensively to this day in movies like *Star Wars*.

As I mentioned before, music can place us into a meditative state, relieving stress and anxiety. It can change a mood—for instance, from happy to sad—or even make you feel energized. In my experience, songs can trigger memories or even set the atmosphere for falling in love. Might it be that real magic lies within the wonders of music?

Inventors have to be futurists, anticipating things or events in the future. I have dabbled in invention, and I hold four patents. I have a dream of being able to play a certain type of music, note combination, or progression that would heal the sick or injured. I used to believe this notion a little ridiculous. Recently, in view of all the wonderful discoveries, I have become optimistic. It might not become a reality in my lifetime, but I believe it is not that far off in the future. I've had this fantasy of healing through playing music for hundreds or even thousands of ill and or disabled people. I can picture seeing people start to smile as their pain disappears, while at the same time, others start to stand up from their wheelchairs. What a wonderful sight and rush it would be to see them able to walk out from my concert, completely healed. I believe that this too, in all probability, will become a reality in the future. I have read many books about the metaphysical universe, and it is said that music holds a key to unlock the mysteries of the cosmos.

Playing by Ear

When I inform my students that I learned to play by ear, they stare back at me with blank yet inquisitive looks on their faces. I had that same look when grandfather said this to me. This isn't covered in how-to books; therefore, I decided to explain this process, and I will do so the simplest way possible. This can be more readily understood after music theory is learned. So don't worry if you can't grasp it, as you can reread this chapter after you've taken lessons.

To me, learning to play guitar by ear was a great help in learning guitar. I wouldn't recommend this to a new student, as it can be somewhat confusing. My grandfather's own explanation was somewhat vague, yet somehow I was able to pick up on it. I make no inference as to whether learning by ear is difficult or easy. It's hard to determine whether this is an innate ability or accessible to all. I have encountered a variety of responses from my students. Some understand, while others are bewildered, and some are in between. You can compare it to writing the melody of a song. Even after listening to hundreds of songs, my first attempts weren't good songs.

I will try to eliminate the confusion by keeping this as easy as possible. After becoming familiar with chords' sounds, you will notice that certain chords are used more often in songs, no matter whether it's rock and roll, blues, folk, or country. Chords like the major, minor, minor seventh, and seventh are predominantly used in all music. Generally speaking, major chords are used more often with faster tempos and hard, punching drive, whereas minor or minor seventh chords are used in slower, mellow songs or ballads and blues. The seventh chord is used in all the above and frequently in jazz. There are now many exceptions, especially when it comes to new age, space, techno, and trance music. Play all the various chords, paying attention to the sounds they present. Eventually you'll acquire an ear for recognizing the variations. Some are subtler than others. For example, the major chord has a straightforward sound; compare this to the minor chord, which has a softer, moody or mellow sound. The seventh and minor seventh are more like a cross between the major and minor chords, with a bluesy or jazzy feel. All of these types of chords will still have their own unique sounds, even when changing keys. Changing keys only lowers or raises the pitch of each chord. These principles apply to all of the other forms of chords, like the sixth, ninth, diminished, augmented, and suspended chords. These are used often in jazz and occasionally in the other genres. Be aware that these chords can usually be exchanged with the other chords above, especially so when playing simple rock, folk, country, and blues.

After learning theory, how everything works will become a little clearer. In the meantime, in order to locate the key (letter name) of the chord, simply go to the sixth string, starting with the string open, and then go up each fret. Eventually you will be able to find the right note, because it will blend in with the music; this is similar to tuning the guitar by matching notes. If the fret you stopped on is the fifth fret, known as the A note, then the chord will be A or a form of the A chord. The form of the chord will have to be determined next. You can play the various forms of the chord until one of them sounds right. This is a process similar to what was described in using the sixth string. As the music moves along, you'll notice that the note or chord you are playing becomes off or sour sounding. Repeat the whole process over again until you have located every chord.

Another method is to follow the bass lines. They need not be exact. Once you think you've got it right, play the bass line and sing at the same time to see if it sounds right. Songs usually use only three to five chords and repeat them, though their order may change, especially in rock, blues, folk, and country. I've run across some songs that were only one or two chords. If you're trying to find lead notes (riffs), you can do this by matching up note for note. Use the same method as done with chords. It is much harder to find lead notes without knowing scales or without the aid of a teacher, but it's not impossible. If you find this too difficult, try finding tablature or learning scales first, like the major, minor, melodic minor, and pentatonic scales. This will help you tremendously when figuring out those lead solo notes we all love so much. Lead guitar is more complicated and may require the help of a teacher or another guitarist. Don't be shy; go and find some help. They can also teach you standard lead patterns derived from scales. These would be of great value too. Unless you use tablature or standard notation, you will still need to use your ears. By the way, not all lead guitar notes are available in tablature or standard notation.

Here's something of interest. All notes can be played against a chord or chord patterns if the notes not in the correlating scale, or odd notes, are played in passing and not dwelled upon. Be aware that you might not be able to match up notes to songs for other reasons. CD players can play at slightly different speeds, throwing off the pitch; they may do so when the batteries start to run down. Radio stations might speed up the songs to fit them in a time slot, although I believe it's not suppose to be done. Some music is actually recorded at a step or half step up or down. You can retune the guitar to accommodate this, but it's a pain trying to match it up. Bending the sixth string by pulling the string can help in finding the right pitch, which will give indication of how much it is off. Sometime there are problems with finding the right chords because the songs are played using open tunings.

Here are some basic rock patterns:

E, A, E, A, B (the bridge or change)
E, G, A (repeat)
Bm, A, G (repeat)
E, A, D (repeat)

These have been used in many songs throughout the years. Rock, folk, blues, and country songs use repetitious chord patterns. There are too many to mention here, and the list of these simple chord changes is long. Of course, there are more complicated songs, but I suggest starting out with simpler ones. As your ear becomes proficient, try more complex songs. The more you endeavor, the easier it becomes, and you'll also start to notice the more subtle chords, like the minor and minor seventh or diminished chord.

I started out learning when rock and roll was young and less complicated. There were only a few artists who used lead solos in their songs. The chord structures were pretty simple too. It wasn't until Hendrix and Page burst on the scene with their blazing guitar licks that guitar took on a whole new complexity. After that, every band worth their salt had a great lead guitarist. The only ones comparable before them were Chuck Berry and, of course, the innovator of the guitar solo, the great Les Paul. Rock and roll and lead guitar is still one big, continuous experiment.

After you have become an accomplished guitarist, experiment with your band's own music. This is how all great artists and bands started out. You'll have to be original in order to stand out. This applies to songwriters and singers as well. Experimenting is a risky business; sometimes you win, and other times you lose, but it's all part of the game. Remember, the great bands and artist become successful by originality. There are what I call "clone bands" emulating the majors, but these never last long. Competition's tough, and only the cream of the crop make it and stay on top. Remember, the music business is all about money. You have to ask yourself on whom would you spend your hard-earned money. The only time I can appreciate a clone band is when the original no longer exists, and sometimes not even then.

When I heard Julian Lennon's music, I thought it was great. After Hendrix passed, it was the same for me with Mahogany Rush and Robin Trower's music.

In recent years, the younger generation has come up with alternative tunings; for instance, there is "dropped D," in which the sixth string in tuned two notes lower. This allows the player to fret the top two or three strings with the index finger, producing heavy-metal power chords. This also facilitates very rapid chord changes. I find nothing wrong with this, but I believe that you should first learn how to play the conventional way. Guitarists in the past have used alternative tunings, allowing them to play unique chords that would be impossible to play with standard tuning. I have also used alternative tunings to come up with a fresh, new sound. Like dropped D, tuning to an E major chord allows rapid chord changes. After doing this, I realized that other rock players had done so before. After changing to an open E major and writing a lot of new songs, I became bored and switched to an E minor open chord. This was very conducive to the new-age music I was writing at the time. It also helped in playing and writing soundtrack music on my synthesizer. Using such tunings as these two enables the guitarist to play lead notes on top of chords easily. Experimentation is the key to success; use it, and it will expand your horizons.

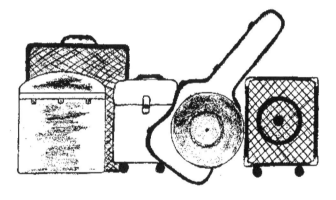

Tips When Playing Out

I thought you would appreciate some tips for when you are playing out. First on the agenda are the strings. I always keep extra sets in my case, along with a couple of extra E and B strings. You should keep a string winder in the case. This comes in handy, especially when a string breaks on stage. Use the extra packs when changing the strings, and don't forget to replace them. That way, you'll have fresh strings all the time. Picks can be placed in several places to assure that there is always one close to hand. I always keep a pick at the top of my fretboard, woven in between the first, second, and third strings and extras ones in my case. Some guitarists keep extra picks under the pick guard and additionally, when playing on stage, several held on a mike stand by double-sided tape. I would consider this a necessity when playing on stage.

Bring extra nine-volt batteries or AC adapters for the effects boxes. Bring talcum powder and hand towels for your hands, face, and guitar. It's always a good idea to wipe down your guitar when you're finished, or after each set. You should also bring along some type of tuning device: a tuning fork, pitch pipe, or an electric tuner.

When playing in foreign countries, don't forget to check on the power source, as you may need to bring adaptors for converting from outlets. I think an emergency kit with over-the-counter medicines is a good thing to accompany you on the road. Here's the short list: aspirin, allergy pills, heartburn and other stomach medications, ibuprofen, and cold and flu medications. These can come in handy on the road, especially if you're about to go on stage. Food that won't spoil and water are good to have too. If you're driving, make sure you have flashlights, extra batteries, an emergency car kit, cell phones, and even blankets and sleeping bags for those long cross-country trips. If it's winter, bring warm clothes and coats; you might even consider camping gear too.

In parting, I have one last story. It's about my first public appearance, and it comes along with a little advice. Our band entered a "battle of the bands" contest in junior high school. The winners would get to play for the coming year's dances. This was my first real public appearance in front of hundreds of kids. Needless to say, my apprehension brought on a case of the nerves. My stage fright was compounded by the fact that I played lead and sang. We were the first ones up, so before the contest started, I quickly ran to the bathroom. In my haste, I broke my zipper, and as you can imagine, I panicked. All I could think of was to get back home and change my pants.

The drummer's dad was there with his car, so I requested that our band go on last. After we got approval, we left, but the traffic was so bad that halfway there, we turned around. I couldn't let my fellow band members down, and I would have to perform with the broken zipper. To complicate things further, while we were tuning up, I ran across a mechanical problem with my guitar and couldn't use it. Fortunately, a friend of mine from another band lent me his.

The time it had taken us to go and return allowed the other bands time to play more than the two songs each band were allowed. But for that, I was grateful. We ran up on stage, and before the curtain rose, I donned my friend's guitar. To my relief, it was much bigger than mine, covering up my zipper. All that ado had been for nothing. After one song, the allotted contest time had run out, so they dropped the curtain on us, saying everyone had to leave. We felt cheated and thought it was hardly fair to us. We had a bad-boy reputation, so as the gymnasium emptied out, we raised the curtain and began our second song. The students started pouring back in, but about halfway through our song, the principal threw down the breakers. We were lucky to only get a strong reprimand.

I felt responsible, even though the others said it really wasn't my fault. But this folly ended on a happy note: we won!

The point I'd like to make here is that when the unexpected arrives in everyday life, don't panic. No matter what, don't panic. Sometimes things have a way of working themselves out. Oh, and by the way, you might want to add safety pins to that list.

References

Kurzweil, R. 2005. *The Singularity Is Near.* New York, NY: Penguin Books.

Noad, F. 2002. *The Complete Idiot's Guide to Playing the Guitar.* New York, NY: Penguin Group.

Randel, D, ed. 1986. *The New Harvard Dictionary of Music.* Cambridge, Mass: Harvard University Press.

Volk, J. 2008. "Sound as the Sculptor of Life." *Atlantis Rising,* May/June.

About the Author

Timothy Sarno comes from a long line of musicians, beginning with his great grandmother, who was a concert pianist. For him, growing up in the 1950s and '60s was a time for fun family gatherings; his grandfather would be wailing away on a banjo while the rest of the family joined in by singing or playing keyboard. The overwhelmingly musical environment of his youth contributed greatly to his decision to play guitar, but he also points out one specific event that really pushed him to play.

While he was watching the Ed Sullivan television show in the 1960s, he was awed by the British invasion of the Beatles. He credits their music and influence with being the catalyst that motivated him to play guitar.

Sarno started off by playing a ukulele given to him by his grandfather; soon, after selling his pool table, he was able to purchase his first electric guitar and amplifier.

Throughout the years, Sarno has written numerous songs with copyrights, performed in rock bands, and recorded studio audio tracks for rock, country, funk, techno, and new age artists. He is an ASCAP (American Society of Composers, Authors and Publishers) member, as both an artist and a publisher. He is also the inventor of the patented Guitar Sweeps guitar picks.